If the Mute Timber

Tom Docherty

If the
Mute Timber

Shearsman Books

First published in the United Kingdom in 2022 by
Shearsman Books Ltd
PO Box 4239
Swindon
SN3 9FN

Shearsman Books Ltd Registered Office
30–31 St. James Place, Mangotsfield, Bristol BS16 9JB
(this address not for correspondence)

www.shearsman.com

ISBN 978-1-84861-809-1

ACKNOWLEDGEMENTS

'Ode to Thomas Tallis' was published in *The Dark Horse*, 40
(Winter & Spring 2019).

'Theory of Tuning Pianos', 'At the Grave of Ludwig Wittgenstein', 'On
Gaudí's Geometry', 'Vespertine Colloquium with a Soldier of the Holy
Roman Empire', 'Poem after a Funeral', 'Spes Scotorum', 'To my Twin
in the Womb', 'The Last Point of Sight', and 'Centoum' were published
in *New Poetries VI* (Manchester: Carcanet, 2015).

'Berg's 'Lulu' Understood at Last as the Interruption of Perfection' was
published in *RAUM*, 2 (2015).

'Theory of Tuning Pianos' and 'At the Grave of Ludwig Wittgenstein' were
published in *PN Review*, 218 (Volume 40, No. 6, July–August 2014).

'Among Birds' and 'Centoum' were published in *PN Review*, 214
(Volume 40, No. 2, November–December 2013).

To Molly

Contents

III

'... in too much light...'

IV

'Name me it, ghost...'

If the sencelesse spheares doo yet hold a musique,
If the Swanne's sweet voice be not heard, but at death,
If the mute timber when it hath the life lost,
Yeldeth a lute's tune…
                    SIDNEY

I

'…Sound in another place…'

Theory of Tuning Pianos

It begins not with a book
nor even an attentive ear.
You have to sit and live with the thing.
You must learn to see grand gestures
in a shiver, discern
each silence of every different moment.

Now place a finger. Be careful:
you are pressing on a beating heart.
Desire to understand nothing that is not
this beating heart. You cannot hear
the equations being made
perfect between two bodies.

Sound in another place. It is yours
to say well- or ill-tempered. Align shoulder
and breast. When time for movement,
move; rest
in the intervals. If your touch is not light,
make light of your thought.

So much is said by the breath
that follows. You are now
at the heart of the way
all this is numbered.
It is imperative you do not speak.
It begins to sound like your lover is awake.

Among Birds

Now is her moment of having nothing
to prove: she speaks only
inwardly as male wings
switch colour, fly and scuff.
The already-defeated sip
at a chlorine pool. All
give the same uninflected hoot:
short-long-short:
an avian amphibrach.
Just one of this rabble is real;
the others hack and mimic, stifling
the air with noise.
A bird emerges.
Neither does he need to prove
a thing, singing to what is
because he is. The tiniest birds
offer obbligato fanfares
to this unknowing purity. Joyous
they tweep and twiff in the freesia.
So the natural king and queen
process, it being theirs to process,
into the palace of sky;
rotating like balloons, children
enter in companionship
with bouncing voices.
The king may not yet realise
but the mocks have died away, foamed
into the distance to leave his hoot,
deep in the red afternoon,
quieter, softer, softening the day,
pleading without desperation
or self-pity. It is a voice so tender
that, hearing it, the other birds
have simply ceased to live,

having nothing to give and knowing
finally what can be given.
It touches everything in the place
without seeming to: the gape
of the moon. Long
after the awaited entrance
it will cry, now nearly dumb,
to balcony and terrace,
across each supine hill's face
and through every window,
only for her ear,
cry over everything
until it has been broken down
to the immortal
mortal
poise of her silence.

Et cultus justitiæ silentium

Is. 32. 17

Milton's *pandæmonium* was for a reason.
He himself compassed
with infirmity in the line
of Homer, past
seeing human face divine,

came to please silence
before returning thence.

Every idle word (I note)
shall be counted in the epilogue
of time. By God. Hope not.
St James had it on the tongue:
a world of iniquity, innate.

Melt down thy gold and silver—
Sirach's abandoned mitzvah—

and make a balance for thy words.
Like marriage, to preserve
what is minted, the quiet works
on us until we can perceive
the coinage it works towards

(of which we have much to say, and hard
to be intelligibly uttered).

Lines on a Birth

Born as we would have had you:
into rain-season, into
a habitation of rain:
to which weeping without strain

can be compared (thus says my
Concise Etymology):
plorare: weep, make to flow:
bound with *pluvia*: rain: so

it makes sense to imagine
a full night's rain at the line
sung in the *Lamentations*
of Thomas Tallis: *plorans*

ploravit in nocte, sweet
against their meaning and yet
a part of it, since we wept
seeing you at last unkept.

Juana Maria

Whether genuinely alone then one
cannot say. Whether to address directly—
without language, genuine knowledge—
is a tongue-tie too. Is you more known or knowing than she?
Easier the probable they who penned her, if anything
like me, scrabbling at the feathers of her dress—
cormorant's—saying nothing of the heraldic cross,
the eating-up eighteen years, or greed.
They said she sang. Invited them in
to her square stanza, four-word, so they heard.
Red her abalone shells for fishhooks. Fetching,
evidently. Taut, to be sure. No line breaks
in her catching smile. All taste and sense
of a tune stripped but not abandoned, scrap
saved, savoured, elsewhere. A leap
out of the line of time
in tones no one
knew.

On the Second of Messiaen's
Méditations sur le Mystère de la Sainte Trinité

With the Trinity to note, even
Messiaen could only imitate
anonymous air-dwellers
(avian and claustral). It is accomplished
imitation. Complete as it has to be.
That kind of embracing
cannot be comprehended.
If a less acknowledged magisterium
were possible, it would be the cloud-
colloquy of wren and blackbird,
transcribed in the one way we can,
which is to say insanely.
More movement in their lines
than anything. *Dieu est saint.*
It is natural. We strain
for the difficult parallel.
Triads played to last.
To a familiar harmony
a yellowhammer chips in:
suis — suis — suis — suis —
suit. The key is awful.
It may not follow to anyone else.

Lyric

I cast off thoughts of you
      to carry through the blue
and hook my mind to what
      trails behind the boat

Then I condemn the wound
      for not being sound

Glencoe

The moor and deer are brown,
unaffected in rain.
Those noble heads are flattering,
and we admire them, enacting
admiration for the deer-like.
We never speak of them: we take
what we have borrowed and we talk
about that.
        We had to sacrifice
our knowledge to become verbose.
To seek what we have been and are,
we gave up on what things were.
We once were deer. We had our calling.
Now we are a different thing.

Berg's *Lulu* Understood at Last as the Interruption of Perfection

Entering then leaving
prison without speaking,
here she is. Snake
like sperm
(everybody loving
himself through her
returning in different dress
even going black
before her clean mirror
through which come
the knife the finger
as if she was never
there   becoming a mess)
          sperm-like
snake—is she here,
speaking without prison,
leaving then entering?

In the Field

The mordancy of birdsong
Reduced and raised him
Gradually, like organum.
The way it opened stung,

This fenestration of sound;
Its leafing-through, its
Leaving. Bugle-call slits
In the wood's sacred wind

Spirited out of pain, dread,
An upward-aiming hurt,
Then a witness to his heart
Growing old; now to the dead.

Ode to Thomas Tallis

I

Spem in alium attests
to exquisite numbers
Thomas tots up, sets
hymning and lets
ring in the *ratio*'s
rafters, the long lift,
left long. Earth's graft,
King's chambers.

II

Man of Lent—strain
per day here—
named, summed,
in recusant pain
across a score.
This counts His
order,
intent on sound judgement.

Spes Scotorum
after Adomnán

I
A VISITATION

MY DRUID was Christ the Son of God. Loved of the Erin
Twelve, I sailed to the salt-main on which the sea-gulls cry,
one grey eye looking back to my little Oak Grove.

After the psalter-battle they sent me on my coracle. So many
men dead for some strokes of a pen, they said. I kept at my
work without compulsion, keeled onto this rock, this Alba.
Ravens stretched over brine.

As a child my fellows were the badger and the pine marten.
Yes, I made water wine, but that was an old trick then; I
preferred picking weeds and thinking at times of time's beauty
and the most naked body.

Back then, fussing with my playthings, I blinked and winds
contrary turned favourable. Look around: you are making
nothing move. Pitiful snoring beast, this is your hour to love.

II
THE DOVE'S HYMN

We____the un - mý _-_ sti - cal have ré _-_____course to__ you

whose name_____is grea _-_____ter than much__

ri _-__chès. You who bróught___the milk _-_____skin

báck____from êbb-tide,_____kéep_____a _-___ way

the waves_____

_____from this_____sà _-___lty__léaf.

A Note to the Tonic

Constant,
I only want
to sound second,
to be re-
conciled to you who
bring me home.
Not making room,

not falling through,
we are stops in air.
Without ceasing to be,
what we are
cannot do:
briefly you must die
that I might live for you.

The line is drawn
To the edge, the end
Of the round
Earth from one side
Of the face
Of which I speak
To the other
On which you are
To whom the line
Is drawn. I draw
The line, beyond
Which I am always
Ending
Up, a way around
The face to one side
Of which I cannot speak.
Not to withdraw
I end sided and spoken
For, the others
Rounded up unfazed
And edged away,
Always beyond
The simple line
On which you are.

II

'…For want of another word'

California, 2015

Age a recurring dream. There is delicacy
in these hands. Their notices.
Not holding the knife tightly.

All country sad in countenance
because nostalgic for Eden. The time between
the taps of the blade.

We are at your mother's breakfast table,
your mother, you, and I. Ends of things
freckle the counter. We eat the last

of your mother's mother's boysenberry jam.

Anecdote

That Christmas your father told the story that used to be

his favourite story about you. There was a general laugh.

Your mother pulled faces with her affectionate eyes.

Someone told you how big the sky is in Alberta

and the turning point of time, God's greatest despair,

though that was untimely. You shuffled in your seat

hearing that man roast his wife, though he remained

smiling. Every time you closed your eyes you felt

some other part of you going to sleep. The turkey was dry.

The old woman from next door who had no children

smiled politely and did not finish her vegetables.

When she offered them, you had at least two of her potatoes.

Some cousin or other of yours kept doubling over

with what you supposed a combination of laughter and nausea.

Apart from the round table, the geometries of everyone

were difficult to make out, though not impossible to shift blindly.

Seems we are always trying to return to a place

we were never in in the first place. Sad in a way

but hilarious in others. And all that. For want of another word.

Robert Lowell

The poet comes round every hundred years
who sings the phonebook. Robert, I am sad
to hear those few stray notes. Too much was made
perhaps of the fun intractable pairs—
1 covered by I on your typewriter.
Too much was said, well, ill, rhyme made unrhymed,
choice made choice lost, the many figures lamed
into one drama. Changing a letter
or two, the dream devoured you, and more.
The great poem you could not write was your death:
what it left out. You ended with a sketch
of an ending in mind; never made clear
whose face framed double in the window-graph,
who named beneath the white unnumbered page.

Appearance of the Lights at Scheveningen and Flood

Anonymous woodcut

Suns in monstrances
condescend yet
no light
to that which goes
disclosed in the almighty
wash
   but keep watch
on the rainbow as beside
the uncompassed steeple
it enters
the sanctuary's heart
        I believe
in a woodcut's theory
presented as the fact it is
   no one owned
its making yet a mark
of flesh at the arc's
root   the remnant
of the tree
all that is here
   what holds it
altogether elsewhere

Voluntary

Aus tiefer Not schrei ich zu dir, but do
Not sing yet: let me feel the organ pang
And ring a little longer, old and new,
In chime with my longing. Outside the strong
Oak cracks, grimaces, unsinewed in ice;
The sun lays down its awful chords, winces.
Holding off, new. At your singular voice
Alone I travel such dissonances.

Diablerie

My knowledge sits loaded
in thirty-five neat shelves
beside my bed,
heavy as bales.

Tonight, with you who binds
my every bookish scrap
together gone,

I worry
      an unread devil,
spirit of mischief,
         spirit of scribbling,
will unhook the hooks,
   unscrew the screws

and send Kierkegaard
      leaping for my temple,
Nietzsche, to behold the man
         and weaken him,
all of Bill to end well
   on my fool's skull,

then Austen persuaded to bite
      my ivory side two inches deep,
Homer with his winedark tome
        to lead me to mine,
Joyce's unfacts feyling after
   by a commodius vicus,
              arseways,

the *Comedìa*
splitting its sides *nel mezzo*
on my nine-circled crown.

But—Goethe yawns in his fall—
is this a devil at all?

Let him push the good book
down on me, and let him speak—
yea, let this snake be heard—
that you may be assured:

I was crushed
by a cunning word.

Ruminants

Follies in nature; no mistakes,
as we mistake it, looking in
from inside. Falling
with the loose cobble, the cat
is at all times achieving
a consummate daftness.
　　Outside a yellow hay bale
cricks like honeycomb.
　　It is here I must be bound,
among lovable things,
lovable because they were so
long ago ordained.
　　My every father
knew by a glance the limits
of butterflies, not self-imposed;
though he might be led
out of his science
by suggestive improvisations.
I add, he knew that also.
　　Where I am unbound
I do not know. I do the done thing
and somehow it is unbeautiful.
Even the disclosure
of my upturned hand
to a passing acquaintance
is enough to condemn
without niceties
my approach to life.
　　And the lovable things
do not love me. They will not.
The cows chew over what they are
to do and do it. I bite on air,
than which nothing better satisfies.
(I eat around the butterflies.)

Feeling Like Tu Fu at the Botanic Gardens

I waited all afternoon for your face
at the cottage gate and then at the statue
of Eve and then at the statue of Ruth
and then at the succulents
you had said reminded you of home.
For the lack of a familiar smile
I wept and wept like an old dog.
In the conservatory everything dripped
with the excess of its own life
without moving. And, which shook me most,
I did not stay to watch for you all day
as I had vowed. But I remembered
the *impatiens*, their white eyes, particle-thick,
wanting for nothing.

On Gaudí's Geometry

Articulate
the governances
of a leaf:
where light,
where water

ribs of xylem
and of phloem's flow
vault the thing,
map it.
The body

communicates.
No drop, no blood cell
stops pool-still
in such
flush-angled

capillaries.

Here in Hiding

Into the path a tree pours leaves.
One bows to the hanging branch and leaves.

In the water each leaf open and close.
The water's path narrow as a close.

Can discuss how heaven's rain will drop down
only so far; only so far rain on the down.

The tree's back broken, that even
the rain breaks; the way it falls, now and then, even.

We arrive at near meanings, and time
is short. All be one in no time.

Disbelieving Spring

You could tell me
there was anything there
and I would believe you
though not perhaps it.

The salty hill
collects dusk.
The winter
waters.

Whatever we have
left, what is left,
is a thing to draw
before,

swaddled or not,
we fade
hysterically
into the background.

Eight Versions of Presence

To an unborn child

And yet then, when the savour of Your ointments was so fragrant, did we not run after You. And so I did the more abundantly weep at the singing of Your hymns, formerly panting for You, and at last breathing in You, as far as the air can play in this house of grass.

—Augustine, *Confessions*, IX, xvi

1

The distinction
between to come,
is persistent
and now and then
I believe that
and will have been
into being.

a field of straw
is marked between
and my word, child.
are, or will not
have known nothing
eye, and your eye.

(says Einstein)
now, and then
illusion
as ever
I have been
watching you

My arms are
No distance
your coming
Yet now you
be, and I
or you, your

43

2

Here I mother and midwife
        you, firstborn (Jonson's offshoot),
on a white sheet. Two-folded
        thing, time's not your compound but
my word. Too much hope of thee.
        I can talk of your nature
no less than that in which I
        live, consider. Are you th'air?
If so, you would open your
        mouth to rain. I am sorry
that I have not seen you. I
        is another story. Not
ink. Doubtful blood. Messy line.
        I do things in my own time.

3

At night I can hear the flock of philosophers,
    the sun nowhere and always
    from east of nowhere,
    compassless true east…

Eriugena's God is not, being gone beyond
    being. *Is* is not a thing
    that is. Forming all
    but out of all form;

superabundant nothing. Quick participant
    in death's charade, you are here
    too, playing I spy
    in the complete dark.

I watch the TV and you. Just static union.
    Prophet-birds: no day so far.
    They announce it out
    of sight: *est*: the sun.

4

I will have been singing
Abide with Me with you
in the future perfect.
Love, how is it you
feel a loss? Who have not been,
who have, are yet
as real as I: and so you will
be gone. Now.

The music is its own
time, outside our measures.
History desists.
Only the countersubject,
subject, exist—
converse. *Amor ipse intel-
lectus est.*

5

Possible no one—
even you—
will
see
what I am
trying to see here.

Is what makes *Hamlet*
tragedy
this
lacked
encounter
with the very flesh?

Who's th'heir. Unimply
yourself. I
play
you
out this way
and stay on the watch.

Ghosts are at least seen.
Stigmatics'
first-
hand
witnessings
to space more pointed.

Blessed interstice,
 I Thomas
blind
doubt
  not the wounds
    where you are maintained.

6

A wind that goeth
and returneth not. Turn
then (the verse is heavily pregnant).
Begin from nothing, a full
moon. Cast being.

Even the handmaid
of God is made with earth.
I'm standing my ground for now. O, joy
is taking the direction
of suffering.

7

I meant to say, this has no direction but it has
                 a point, a *punctum*, around
which it reels elliptically. Time-dishonoured
Ptolemy had one too, the equant.
You, somebody I guess, may come about by me but I'm not
                          your centre.
You're watching the eccentric X God already deleted
on my blank verso of sky.

Turning it over to music, the punctuated
                 breaths that look a trace like stars,
asterasters—hold that incomplete note tied—
indefinitely hard to pinpoint.
I try to remember the asterisms, every
                          now and then.
Before your aster mouth opens, I'm all right with three pointed
things. You, crossed love, and the dark.

8

When my grandfather died, the rosary
    was said. More than one time
lines crossed, beats overlapped.
A wee boy, I could hear
my mother's heart: no other
proof needed. *You* is a rhythm

and the first gift. A rhythm, to repeat.
Je dors, mais mon cœur veille.
    How do I have you now,
virgin birth? A vigil
at a painting. There the Christ
Child rests in her robe as in her

flesh and looks. There is no one else in sight.
The scene of constant hills
    and the mother's watch. Her
hands praying a hill, hair
endless tresses. This language
without ingredient and grave

a tent of presence. His arms outstretched
to take the empty hill
    and stand in that nothing.
I thirst the last blessing
and end of exposition.
The word finished being given.

Raining in Hamilton

The plants in my hometown are green,
weedy, immersed, too bled into
my mind. Anywhere
    a weed can grow.

The dark leaves impelled through the burn
twitch like wet scavengers.
A white bungalow
    smokes gently.

Everything carries the water
in what way it can; each absorbs
the soft weight
    until it must yield.

Since freedom is to restrict what threatens
freedom, I should praise the weed
for drowning, the ink
    for staining the page.

Poem After a Funeral

Rhotic tremble
of a bee

in the garden's last
summer wind:

I tell it
of an old family friend

who also
swallowed spring.

III

'…No revelation and no gaze…'

Dawn in Cambridge

Smurry. Undistinguished rain.
There is no element of wind in the eaves.
To all such and nonesuch
undomiciled this unrefined
definition.
Once no want of contact, from there
suitable eventuals.
Almost all, even
the purest-gilded, birdsong.
First favours of morning.
The grove-window set back
in its place, hushed by shrub.
Time is set aside for all this
beautiful refusal.

At the Grave of Ludwig Wittgenstein

Not death but overgrowth. Gorgeous
throat of earth, excess of abyss:
I see the stumps of trees and raise
them the constellation-branches,
a second nature's necklaces,
and this, a string of sentences
but not. This strings what I invent.
I have no idea where you went.

Snowy Landscape at Éragny, with an Apple Tree

Camille Pissarro, 1895

It is impossible to say
    whether I am at the top
        or the bottom of the hill.

        The sky is an old scroll
      fringed orange
   where a sipped sun spilled.

Apple eyes violet and leaf
   sees bush sees peach.
      The morning got punched

        and I am seeing a star
      leak, like (so to speak)
  a blacking eye.

Piette's House at Montfoucault: Snow Effect

Camille Pissarro, 1874

Snow and sky: a greening grey.
House and tree: an effluence,
a deep and dark becoming, marks in grey.
Everything is asleep
in too much light.
The trees are big children frozen
in play. Light, but not dazzling:
light that is like shadow: light
of constant suggestion: suggestion,
but never fulfilment.
The light has no body
and does not desire one.
What is behind it is nobody.
An indent, a little new-made snow-valley,
corners the house. Horses
I imagine have walked there.

To my Twin in the Womb

You face away from me in the sailing bed
Cut granite stays course
The rain follows me uphill
Flowers examine the field

We are made in water we are made
To feel we are not made to exist
Ranunculus abortivus
I daresay I will wait here awhile

Transfiguration

Three stars nailed into Kirkwood air:
I think of your briery hair.

The sky is full of whips and slaps.
Trudging uphill. Your long steps.

The awful awareness of a skull.
One pushing arm feels the other pull.

One arm holds a hand, its father's;
one hauls the unwitting splinters.

To ask what the sky is promising
is to reveal what one is missing.

A hyssop drips from sky to mouth.
The banquet-wine on your breath.

Three nails in the Kirkwood air.
It is wonderful for us to be here.

Vespertine Colloquium
with a Soldier of the Holy Roman Empire

Well of course the *imperium* will implode!

It teaches rebellion by conquest! We start in blood and botulism
    but we end in books. Pinakes and ciboria sprout
    from Aachen to Saint-Denis; we make bedposts
    for love's sacrifice Misericords
    relieve us, first *in ecclesiam*, then of our enemies *in agro*.

Barbaric? You mean foreign. To conquer with order
    is a gift. The genitive belongs to you now.
    Here are our cases, where
    do you keep the drink? You can have no picture
    without a frame—ours (it's plique-à-jour).

Long live Charlemagne and Charles Martel's mantle.

The Königspfalzen cry out *Pater Europae* (not
    quite a paternoster); crepuscular
    rays reach the emperor's robes.

Alcuin's mind is English and delectable: *vox populi*, he knows,
    is Christendom by morning and whoredom
    by mid-afternoon. But Eriugena's brain is Irish
    porridge, not worth its salt or salary.

What I take is what a lover takes. The soldier's pay
    is a warm reception. The poet says
    nos quoque per totum pariter cantabimur orbem
    iunctaque semper erunt nomina nostra tuis
    —yes, even your names for yourselves
    will be entwined with ours, even
    the raindrop names in night's parched vale (*vale*).
    You will be sung *sub voce*, a few cents
    under our tongues.

But at *Completorium*, remember these are interludes.
    I saw a thousand men fall at my side,
    and ten thousand more at my right hand.
    They will not be remembered.
    I am trying to give, not to take. These few valiant
    are tympana, archivolts for the *tabernaculum*,
    where the building is not my notion or yours.

What did he say? *glorificabo*. Come on in.

April Running

You read a river home. Larch
and beech follow.

Often I imagine your knees
against the bulrushes.

Remnants

I

Seams of water self-dug into hoar-frost;
the earth seems freshly broken.
Bony clumps of sedge
deliver their regalia of twindles,
humble garlands speckled white.
The sun spreads its jagged
skirt over the whole scene.

II

Sugared brambles verge the farmlands;
spruces stand tight-packed, primed;
their effortless faces.
            A stone in grass. Red
shag heaps. Here and there in the trees,
unsteady oblations
of copper and amber.

III

Further, dirt shed for a slip road
rich as horse manure,
not to mention the islands
of refuse everywhere
planted,
as though in ordained
dwelling-places.

Port

Seen just at the violeting of day,
sleepy, loose-fingered, the short port town
nictitates and yawns small-ly.
The cottongrass is folding itself down.
Doodles of sedge stretch, unravel all
down the flickery bank of the knoll.
The no-noise is like hardly-hindered breath
from an unnoticed nose.

No revelation and no gaze
will make a thing move in a haven this aloof.

Spanish Sketch

Ice-cream-scoop clouds stacked.
Stalks of fruit tall
against each other.
The hens are small.
The chickens are small.
Smaller than I can see.
Yet this is hen-and-chicken land;
look how they peck like
they're the only ones in the field.
I can't even see them and they are
the only ones in the field.
They speak in Cervantes voices
and are long forgotten by their ancestors.
They're too small to eat fruit
and can't decipher anything in clouds.
What becomes of them will never be
discussed, though people
conjecture back and forth forever.
When they make eyes, which is whenever
they have the chance, one of them
hastens time forward and the other daydreams
of water
from white clouds
into a field
for patient soil.

Suzanne Valadon, 1923

The artist models: the seen sees:
there are skins between self and self.
She lies upon some leaf or shelf
of her own making, at her ease.

In paint she is neither Suzanne
nor Maria, her stare no one's,
as no one's there to entertain.
She thinks of those she knew once.

Francis Bacon, 1971

Black lines divide the man
    and the truth of the man.
Black desolate as white.

He is hardened into cloaks,
    violently becoming.
Time or thoughts pass: his face flies.

Some may remember half a mouth,
    an eye glazing to marble,
how his hair wept. To anyone he is foreign.

Sick of the composing
    and the being composed, he
is a sentence spurning words;

the sky greater
    and less congruous through windows,
he makes himself unrealer than the world.

For Rockroses

The wrinkle-petalled rockroses
are too vulnerable to live, and yet
they are this island's purple
and its pink. They will be happy
to meet death, being already old women
and tired of all this light and heat.
The imminence of something is too intense;
one cannot be content in this weather.
I love you, rockroses, because you are weak,
and because you are not ashamed
to be afraid of the world around you,
and because you are wrinkled
and teach without having words,
without having.

...

Loved ones, have you inherited
my falsehoods, the failures
I seem to pass on in secret?
This lying legacy infects
even the sky and trees, withering
as they struggle to remember
how they were originally conceived.
I've heard that trees are only trees;
but we humanise the foreign,
and this is not true consolation.
So, Catalina, Catalina Tomàs,
can I pray to you on your land,
not being on your sea?
Can I pray to you for landsickness?
Dear Laura Riding, you lived here too
and failed to reconcile your love
with its lie; can I pray to you

for my poor poem,
that it may be also poor in spirit?

...

It is easy to overreact
to one's own wretchedness,
the unbearable every gesture
and remark, since on what skin
has the sun not left its sign?
Probably it is our way of clinging
onto that simple lie, telling ourselves
it is insurmountable, though its shape
is always changing. My father's shadow
crooked and dwindled down the corridor;
I was glad not to know what he was thinking.
I nipped a long-dead fly with my pen's nib:
it crumpled like hard dirt. No mustard blood.
I went to bed. The familiar
uncertainty. It is easy to forget
that *do not be afraid* is not a reassurance,
but an order at odds with our being.
Through the slatted window,
the cars rolling by three floors up;
next door the pulse of snoring;
and the not-there orchid smell.
The comforts, stranger antidotes
to strange poisons. Sometimes it helps
to be reduced to five senses.
I see, then, I have developed something
of a tan. Have mercy.

...

Wise and silent but not asleep
in the respite of dark. Old women,
buds of Peter, do not abandon this rock:

you are its colour and its voice,
disorientation's cure,
the boat of the land; where you are
there is the hope that something can be
full of deceit and full of truth,
only while you are here, dying
between the orange trees and the lemon trees.

IV

'Name me it, ghost…'

Prayer

Name me it, ghost,
the thing not lost.

A Prayer in Coltness

I

To church, as they did.
Snow illuminates the dead
branches, each at once defined.

II

A step out of the way of things,
into a permanence that strings
along besides. The law it brings

III

to mind: the land is held
of the King. It's called
a dominion, m'lord, and leaves me cold.

IV

So I to what is real.
The true myths continually roll,
occasionally unreel;

V

settled for a time, may
they, like snow impressing the may
with God's face, mark at last me

VI

when my May has come and gone.
To church, as they did, again.
Snow illuminates the grain.

Centoum

from Les Murray

I walk on home where the stars are thinnest, glancing
the dented light of milk cans.
I will wake up in a world that hooves have led to
the edge of dark country. I could not afford

the dented light of milk cans
in winecellar towns at peace with their horizons.
The edge of dark country I could not afford
hangs over me moveless, pierced everywhere by sky.

In winecellar towns at peace with their horizons,
the tree grows troubled, trembles, shifts. Its crown
hangs over me moveless, pierced everywhere by sky.
On a landscape wide as all forgiveness

the tree grows, troubled, trembles, shifts its crown.
I walk on home where the stars are thinnest, glancing
on a landscape wide as all forgiveness.
I will wake up in a world that hooves have led to.

To the Architect of the House of the Lord, Who Though Wise Came to a Doubtful End

I

The Wisdom literature has a bit
of the dry comedian about it—
even in *anger is better than laughter*,
or *the heart of fools where there is mirth*, after—,
carefully slapdash books of wit.
Handful of pains wryly lit.
The grandest admissible writ.
That orders you to be a grafter.

II

And graft one *lingua* to the next—
but be apprised: this surfeit
of tongues is no gift, but a forfeit,
and laws' lacunae injury of text.
Non liquet. There are no words
but *the law of the Lord is unspotted*,
the cellar of wine where we're seated
justified, offering its own rewards.

III

He set in order charity in me.
Back in the right place. Flowers of the field,
set about with spines, love justice and yield
immaculate simplicity.
I must be, then, a fox that strips the vines,
caught up by Christ the gardener.
Heart, soliciting clobberer,
thank God your pardoner without these lines.

IV

Do not confound yourself. You muddle
no less now than ever, and no worse.
The syntax of your thoughts is still perverse,
the prime: no primmer. Justice immortal.
The very word—hypocrite—chokes me.
Becoming autobiography,
Solomon: and if I die quickly
turn me to your verse before dirt takes me—

V

as it ought, for honouring *inventions
of art, and the resemblances of beasts*;
errors kept as laws, doubtful intentions
turned undoubted villainies: so wastes
the state in me. *Commandment of tyrants*
to gawk up to figments, contrivances;
a holocaust of infants, convenience;
and, just where their praise should be, silences.

VI

Don't you laugh, preferring a hidden picture,
*the sight whereof enticeth the fool to lust
after it, and he loveth the lifeless
figure of a dead image*? Such brightness
shade on shade thrown. Dear Lord. I trust
you yet recall dread Pharoah's measure.
The plagues now seem to kill souls just.
Names double as wild swarms—conjecture.

VII

God's words, too great for ours, split them.
The best end remarried with mixed
expectancies, pride having quit them;
grown up in fear, in age are fixed.
Tramp your word in soil for its worth,
the way of humiliation
its testing ground. See if its birth
crack stones in God's or earth's nation.

VIII

What happened then in Egypt was unclear
to no one. Two tablets dropped for pity's sake.
So much for the soil. The word the fear
inspires. Therefore it is no mistake
Aaron's holy robe was *a wise man's*
woven work, endued with judgment and truth;
no shock it took God's lapidary's hands
to etch its gems, eye for eye, tooth for tooth.

IX

All deepening into affinity.
Draw me: we will run after thee
to the odour of thy ointments.
The broken alabaster makes amends.
One stick to another as bones.
The word is *reditus*, and courts the mind
Tabernacled elsewhere, as though it found
That house the brickings-up of which are bonds.

Stanzas towards an Artefact

i

When they tore the robes from Him,
it was to pierce a monstrance:
His immaculate veil. Mary; Mary's.
To wrap it up, she fashioned Him. A Son
always dressed to the world
by His Mother God of her stitch.

ii

They tore the robes whose tassels
a bleeding woman touched:
the tassels were the seal of interwoven Law,
and He who wrote it wore them.
Who hath touched My garments?
He did not ask it of the soldiers, being unread.

iii

Robed Word,
what You retain in skin itches
to wear the cuts they made,
to bear that dismantling
that I be red in gold.
Lord, clothe me in what Your Mother sewed.

M. M. M.

Os suum aperuit sapientiæ, et lex clementiæ in lingua ejus.

Anxious to begin, little hardly significant
breaks in
composure, oh how I want to say the word here
darling: and double it
each time you echo her
flutter of sibilants, stops, teaching the works once they are
gone, how I want to say the word
how, but you have her wild
intelligence and have beaten me to it,
just, and knowing her absent of I is
knowing her, and you do. You are her mother.
Letting the shallow utterances
mean something close to
not meaning something, you
open and close,
prize them, as they opalesce.
Question: was Solomon's mother the wisest?
Reasonable to ask after this long.
She didn't go halfsies on anything;
though I can't help thinking of you, nude
under shade outside, it's not inconceivable, though
visibly not enough shade.
What's too much to imagine is us conversing,
xystus-shaded, longer than an unstifled
yawn, length of a languid
zinnia she in her bonniness took from you.

A Dedication

Further white with cloud, nearer white with rain.
Birds voice insistently against
the steady rhythm of rain on full grass. The morning appears
to have stayed all day. You have gone out, with my mother,
to try on wedding dresses. I am supposed to be working.
Brahms's Intermezzo in A ghosts my consciousness.
How comfortable one can be
without the tonic. Clearer than gin this comfort.
How did he who had no dream of heaven dream this heaven?
And yet not heaven, not yet: the sublime has a line;
what it says is beyond it.
You can't reason that out
which satisfies. The rain has halted, the birds have reached
grand polyphony. I was wrong, the puddles are still rippling.
The part about the birds was right, right
enough. The sky hasn't changed.
This an intermezzo that doesn't connect anything.
To make something perfect is alone a perfect ending
at which one never arrives. Come
near with me, love.

Song

Of Samuel—L.—I sing
and Aristotle who stalled
before the word—

Churchill to whom so much
so many would say would be ode—
and that guy from *A Fish*

Called Wanda. A tetra-
grammaton transposed
in 'the heart of light,

the silence' of any
quartet of chords,
a life's leitmotif

(but Messiaen found
no letters
in reply to God's);

all men
insignia
of spit

daubed on dirt.
I stick with Lavinia
who printed 'sorrows plain'

(note the tautology,
even, in that).
O numbered One

who can account
for the marks
we leave

saying only that they are—
enjoined to the—
inarticulacy of—

God I fancy,
to whom I consign
my infancy.

A Registration for the Feast of the Annunciation

i

Unfigured
ground bass
of His
Humanity:
Baixo, pedal
reed, some depth,
its own bare line
not unworthy
of display.

ii

Dry and sweet,
the rest tuned
to it: note,
new word,
the beatitudinous
Octava:
His Divinity.

iii

Not mere
pondering
Fourniture,
this *Mixtur*.
Fractal-
mosaic of Man.
Delta harmonics.
Absolutely

singular
Copula.
This mutation's
unheard of.

iv

So inappropriate,
the *Regal*
en chamade. Whoever
conceived of it.

To my Four-Month-Old Child Asleep

One night you will not
be consoled by my hand's mere
quasi-divine weight.

A Conjugal Prayer

Efflorescence called out
　　long years askance,
calyx and a sexy dance
　　with tilt of bee,
a mixed marriage.

O held among the saints,
　　lost or unsent here,
felled at the last, let fail
　　in uncalled-for
appalling April hail,

another funeral. Set sail.
　　Must end soon.
All the fallings-out baffle me
　　and see me off,
key in the wrong door, whistling

a battered tune. Men mourn
　　the death of a husk,
not of its hidden mutables.
　　Give them height
and depth, not a cloud to jig with.

Kinged and ringed, latter-day Louis
　　Quatorze catching
sunlight, his plaything, the jingle
　　of keys golden
and sharp—*diabolus*—self-made

homunculus, his little finger sharp
　　to point it out
(no dissonance allowed). Rameau
　　wraps up, *clavecin*
closed, no room to gild guilt

with unaccompanied and godly
    final cadence.
In the unperfect garden the dandelion
    wilts of its own accord,
dulling each slat of unstained grass.

In words of the Holy Shepherd,
    qui legit, intelligat,
nation nears ruin. The temple trembles.
    Abomination
of desolation. Cleft wax and all else still.

Wickedness ours alone. The animals
    beautiful, *fuori le mura*,
but ours tribunal, tribulation,
    cum tuba et voce magna,
awful bell, jarring earful.

I did not forget demons. They drew me
    from the start. Their evil
lacks tragedy: choice, but no chance,
    fugue state not stated,
nothing unsaid because nothing said.

Instead: sweet counterparts, gather
    from corner and fold
unfeeling, coarse, unknowing us,
    annul what falters
and fends us. Anneal us lukewarm

weaklings unconcealed. Rock bottom
    drilled through
to cordial mettles met. Last ditch
    touchdown: no need
for mediation of accidents. The body true.

Testimony

Unaware what reasonable people do
for the summer, here we are in the graveyard
of a small college town in northern Utah.
Sun, corpses, poplars.

We hide from the light and dark both. We finish
up walking from and from. Yet here we are now,
flitting daws. The grass is meticulously
Christian, and bespeaks

its nation. A wild plot gives it up for earth,
overpraises its own heady recklessness.
Where's Adonai to walk in the cool of day?
These dead are marked out,

crossed off, defiantly unassimilate.
We stay on gravel, scanning names for double
entendre. That they be heard again. We find
some real miracles.

The same ground naturally gets worked. The same
goes in as came out. Irony: we're the ones
in the dark. What damnable jokes. If they know,
they know yes or no.

We make our ways out, all the time between shades.
Like children who have fallen and scraped their knees,
we get ice cream. The poplars, remember, were
Balm of Gilead.

An Engagement Present

Beauty! In lily,
daisy, phlox.
Maybe a dot moth
spent the night
among them;
and morning glory.
You their queen.

I wanted our love to be a Christ-child,
made visible in a stable.
Strange delivery.
You, taken wondering
by this, which was always to be.

The mark borne greatly
on your body.

The Last Point of Sight

Yes, only one star is visibly here
tonight and yes, it is saying
then, then, then like a white dog
and it is saying *before you were born,*
saying *I was before you were born,*
before you or any of this was thrown
knock-kneed into a struggle for breath, I was
and you do not know if I am anymore,
wild grasses along the roadside
are nodding heavily in sad, old-man agreement,
every little blade visibly agreeing,
though at different times, and in varying frequencies
according to the heft of each single heave;
and yes—continuing from my street
along and slowly down the blue-black oak hill
and over the stone bridge over a pebble burn
to the next family of lights—
the end of the fencepost trail
and the end of the line of the curves
are always evading the last point of sight,
which appears to say
continue, to say
follow like a dog or a man
led by a dog, since you do not know where you are anymore;
and yes, okay, the star is even blinking now leg-tremblingly
as if it was a shivering old man before there were old men,
to nail its point into the sky,
to repeat for now and tonight the word *fragility,*
appearing to curve a visibly broken line

and yet all that travels beyond it is now
will we continue to love
though we remain
heaved and blind and not yet born.